Even the Oceans had A Story to Tell

SETHULAKSHMI KB

To those who embrace the emotions of the

human heart

Preface

To my readers

Wabi-Sabi

Preface

Poetry is the art of expressing the emotions
of the unheard or

sometimes the penned presentation of
human thoughts

walking through the bridge of souls
travelling to nowhere and seeking quite nothing
of concern

yet bagging a huge pile of cores of millions
providing them tranquillity, passion, despair and
ebullience of one human element to get
passed on to another.

This opus of mine is not something of great
praise when compared to other books but still

holds a bundle of wordings you were scouring
for to enrich your inner souls with a warm

blessed umarmen and peace to your cruise of
Sanguine Fluid.

To My Readers

Many a time back in my school days, I felt like "She dances so well", "His song is too adorable", "She's a pure genius in academics and calculations", "They are the cheetahs of our class", and many more. And to ponder upon myself I had only "Why am I not good in all these... Why do I not have any such special flairs like them..... And it felt desperate throughout my life, realising I couldn't excel in anything and I was just a normal human indifferent to others. Until, one day my class teacher, who was supposed to be teaching Hindi, brought up with the idea of giving her students an assignment concerning the last taught chapter. She knew little that one of her students from the 7th Grade (Her own class) would later become a writer. Her thought of bringing up a poem self-written by her pupils struck my head and entire body to freeze as if I were in the

Eastern Antarctic Plateau since I knew that I was the weakest student in her subject from the entire class as I even wrote my Hindi exam twice just to get failed twice. Grateful to God that I managed to pass it every year in my final exams. I was so frightful that I considered it better to make someone else write it for me. Luckily, I found none to fulfil my purpose. Then I thought, why shouldn't I give it a try? Maybe I would fail or it would turn out to be nothing more than a piece of jumbled words, but at least I gave it a try. Hence, I grabbed my pen, took out a flat unlined notebook from my table, sat down on my veranda staring at the raining cats and dogs and the thunder and lightning followed by it. Hurray! It played out to be something of not bad vibes, giving me hope that at least it had meaning. Later on, I found it quite interesting giving me a mind of satisfaction and pleasure. Moving on further in this path scribbling more and more, experiencing Kaizen from devising scratches to forging artworks that convey emotions, now I got to look back and realise yeah, I wasn't that of a common kid. This 21-year-old would like to recount a message to that 12-year-old - "Every knack is exceptional and captivating. But the art of creation is not that simple and not everyone gets it. It needs vivid imagination, extreme care for the emotions of oneself and others, and most significantly, you must be considerably fortunate that God gives you his magic wand to spread the hymns of words."

From your author

1. Your Eyes

I saw your eyes yelling those secrets

That you have kept as a russet

I know you treasure me

But I can't push you.

All I can do is Stare at your deep brown eyes

With a million stories

That I hold back to myself

To keep you even more loved.

The light I saw in your eyes

Was never seen anywhere

The stories you tell me through your eyes

Was never heard before

That I get sunken in those eyes

To melt myself in pain

When I know this's all in vain

2. Player

I said this ain't sensible

But you never heard me

I voiced this won't work out

But you didn't believe me

Now we ended up like strangers

From a very valuable bond

Now you're not mine

And I can feel that

You played a game

Which I wasn't much interested

And now you left the game

Making me wedged within the bounds of it

You were a good player

But I am not

3. From Strangers to Family

We never knew that we were making moments

That would last forever

Even though it faded with time.

Friends for a lifetime

Was discovered from the oceans

That carved on

'Unity and Discipline

Those smiles, those cries,

Those sparks, those Josh.

Macras everywhere

Even seniors turned out to be

The coolest of all!

Those unending mess queues

6 o'clock and roll call.

"It's idali or dodali ?

I don't know have it!"

"Arrey yeh bend hai!

And I said Neeche Byte!!"

And it all wrapped up for

The 'Paanch minute ke liye line thod!"

Those heart-whelming screams

For your BN or Group

Those screams that you'll never miss

Even if your throat has died

Pushups that you took together

Not for sin but for Josh.

Those eye-catching fights and

Those breathtaking result proclamation
moments

And it all wrapped up for

To make one of the finest packages

Of God's creations

Turning out total strangers

To a single family

Under a common shade of light

Called NCC!

When it's a feeling

Not a chore.

4. Juliet's grief

How can I tell you that

I love you more than anyone else

But I want you to stay away from me

Cause I will break your heart

And burn it into ashes

With a split of time

But I still want you to hold my hand

For a lifelong

Can this happen even in our deadly dreams

I'm trying harder and harder to forget you But
still you come up like phoenix in my wildest
dreams

Burning the pebbles of the door I closed
Making me deeper to build the door even
more stronger... How can I tell you that

I love you more than anyone else

But I'll harm you

All the images used within are not created by the writer

When I want you even more closer

I know I'll throw those triggered bullets

right through your heart

I know I'll clash all the castles you just made

for me

Cause I'm an augur

Veiled up in a cover

With all the pricky thorns

That you dare to touch

Even in your death aura.

Cause baby you don't know that

I float over the Red Sea

That people even dare to see

Cause baby you don't know that

You are following a crazy little elf

That has got a shelf

With a load of altered self

And you should know that I love you That I

would break those filthy barriers just for you

And still say I hate you For

the sake of you.

5. The Fairy Meraki

You make me cry, you make me laugh

You make my heart melt like an ice-cream

You make my day, you feel like me But

on a twisted round ago.

The way you smile

The way you fight

The way you just don't talk to me.

Eyes that sparkle

Locks like marbles

Flying as a fairy girl

Look into the window

You just gotta daydream

Oh! She is here

Lemme peep in through

Yeah, she is the girl that ever twisted me.

A dedication to my friend Sneha

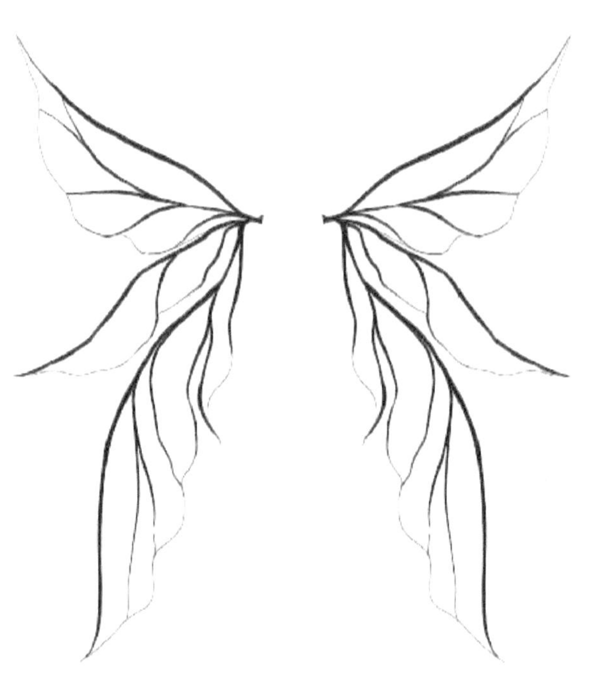

6. Wanna be with you

Sometimes I feel like

I wanna be with you...

Then I look and realize

That you are okay without me

The smile on your face

Make me realize

That an end has happened to this phase.

Somedays I feel like

Talking to you

And then I realize

That your life without me Is

on a good case.

Those deleted messages,

Those unanswered calls...

I'm trying to forget everything

When it all feels like

You are okay without me...

7. The Unfinished Hope

You my sunshine

I know you never cared

But still, I wanna be with you

It pains so hard

When I realise

That you are not mine...

I feel so empty when you move

afar

But still....

Mon coeur t'appartient

May not be mine

Might be the 'mine'of someone else

I know you never cared

But still, I wanna be with you

Just wanna live a life with you

Cause I'm the one who feels kefi

When you umarmen

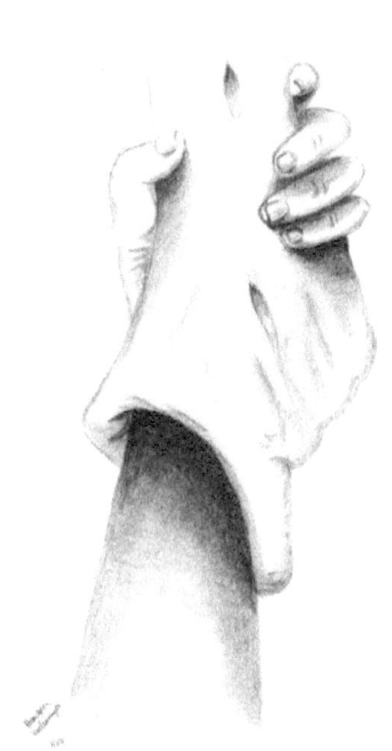

And you know the reason...
That you are the soul of my wounded heart

The raison d'être of my mortality

You make my demonic days angelic,

My silhouette shine bright

Even at night

And my death a worth.

And you are my love

I know you don't care

But still, I wanna be with you

Maybe you are not mine

I know my perception of you

Is a kalopsia

But you are my nirvana

8. Aurora

You are the peace

That I was digging for.

The essence of purity

That frame the inner me.

You keep my spirit up

And feel my pang

You are mine,

Just mine and mine.

I'm in deep devotion

With these soulful winks

Of the ticking time

My peace and joy Is

who you are.

I am the moon

That bounds around you

And you are the day spring

That drives me in

Let me take it high and pure

To the field of adoration

9. And Still You Couldn't Know

You are a fantasy

That I crave every time

When I feel like I'm lost

You are that thing

That leads me to a winsome promenade

That I have unperceived

Are you an enchanted petal from the past?

Or a present of the present?

You are carved on in my veins

For a kiloannum

Even the fallen leaves

Sing about this magical love of us.

And still you couldn't know...

I know you exist

But where can I find you

In the lane of memories

That I brought
Or in the allured valley that awaits for me

10. Sin

The grief I hold
Is heavier than my soul
I have been waiting for ages
Meeting several sages
To close the hole
Found in my soul

The sun is dark

And that's a mark
The night shall swallow
Making it hollow
Through the deeds
Of the peeps
I have lived
Still living
Will continue to live
In the Dil of
Of the ill
Sin am I
Sinner am I
Seeking grace
Without a face
Making trace
Through these ill faces

11. Cruise of Sanguine Fluid

I have been lost in your thoughts

But that loss

Was all fine for you

Cause you knew

That this was all a thrill for you.

I was crying and dying

Begging your attention

When you enjoyed

Making me your fan

A cease to my bruise,

Peace to my cruise

Is all I want

Getting back myself

Being in verisimilitude

Is what I'm building right now

Moulding back my inner phase

Where you are not a part

12. Rope that Bleeds

I'm your second choice

Yet you are my only choice

Voices are telling me

Drop it out and move on

My heart is no more for you

Yet I can't break this rope

That is tied

From my heart to yours

I'm trying hard

Hard and hard But

what I get is vain

After all this pain.

Was I a void?

Daily being toiled,

To keep this cheloid...

Just to get spoiled

By your false heart.

I can't force this anymore

Cause I am forcing myself to the grave.

Giving my heart to you

When all you do is

Proving me wrong

I can't force this anymore

Cause I am forcing myself to grave

13. Spectre of Ephialtes

Your crooked thoughts have been killing me

Penetrating deep into my soul

Bleeding my inner wounds of memory

That I slowly sealed with sorrow

You ghosted me more than thrice

And now you have come up

As a ghost in my ephialtes.

I never craved your attention

But you gave

And when I asked for

You treated me like I don't exist

The ghost that I never wished to be

ghosted by

Is now ghosting me day and night

For real and for illusion

Your deadly mouth is engulfing me
Spraining my spine and brain

Slowing the pace of my every breath

Where I gave my heart

It was made into shapes of blades

thinking it to be clay

The wooden stone kept barely

inside my ribs

That I thought was killed years

back

Is now aching for no reason

You are draining me in and out

Through my soul

With your pointed pendant of words

Cutting myself into ashes.

Rejuvenation has become harder I realise

when I feel this as Sielvartas

14. Amoureux

How hard it feels

As your ears are engulfing the warmth

Of the fresh blood pumping

Inside the cone-shaped flesh

Of this masculine body of mine.

The beats of music within this beast

At the highest and closest.

Holding your arms in mine

Hoping this is not a Sundreesoro

Yet all I can do is

Watch at your glazing iris

Feeling the melody sung by the

Mesmerizing human art you have drawn

Within the flimsy impediments of your

heart room

Shut and locked with the strongest doors

Kept secret and securely

With whom you walk through miles

Speaking nothing in huge

Even so with an emotion of great joy

And of querencia

How hard it feels

When you are the meaning

of the zephyr

Flowing through my nares.

I being the valley of tranquillity you

abide by

Though the story of the one above

Glorifies us to dive in through

Two different walkways

Never being allowed to flow together.

The melancholy inside me

Is tearing up myself

Painting the leaves of the

Twain Protruding orbs of this fellow one

With salted Adam's ale

15. Euphoria

You are the shadow that I bloom on

You ain't my Euphoria,

Yet this feeling is historia

The world is all I have on

And that world is you.

The fear of losing you

Is my biggest nightmare...

I am not perfect

I do have scars

But you are the heal to those scars

You are the shadow that I bloom on...

I am a believer and my faith is you

I thrive to live for you.

You are the shadow that I bloom on.

16. The one who came to smultronställe

The time tides I shared with you

Was a waste of time

Yet the feeling of regret

won't deluge me

Cause I made a lesson

That I won't forget

An epiphany that the care and compassion,

The sparkles made by the sprinkles of love

Are all beautiful only when it lasts for a

lifetime.

You engraved this bitter truth on the

delicate walls of my heart

Turning it into a pictured portrait

Which is no longer alive

To feel the same for you.

The eternal tranquillity of heaven

Have embraced it lovingly
Embarking it with the embroidery of

immortality

That delicate piece of tissue that was

Securely stored inside the strong bones

Of this human form of art of the

heavenly Is now just a piece of rock

Punishing itself every bit of time

17. La douleur exquise

How long will you hold this pain

That I still see in your pictured heart

The tacenda passed between us

Is still a kalopsia

And I'm feeling anagapesis.

As it says

"Shikata ga nai"

Our mizpah was a beautiful gluggaveour

Only to be enjoyed behind the

Windows of our cores

You are still aching in Oneirataxia

When both are getting toska

This is 'La douleur exquise'

Let the marmoris come up

Making our hearts no longer ache

You were my nepenthe

But now a magoa

18. Que Sera Sera

"Breaking your peace

Is my hobby"

Said he without a glance

Making me abash

Rethinking myself

Should I really get him into my life?

19. Core

"This cold is tightening me

Freezing the core within

This hoar is hard to break

The Inferno bound in me

Is nowhere to be seen

Bits of moments from the early

I remember strongly

The large roars of my blaze

Melting the tiny piece of ice

I met accidentally

The cold trembling breeze around you

Fading into the air to see none

Each hearted step of yours

Vanishing into the ocean of fire-red

Oh my beloved

Where has your mesmerizing heart gone?

Your loss is now tempting me to death

Strong breezes of timid ice

Is engulfing the tiny red dots

Inch by inch
Turning it shallow and unseen

Was this a war of vengeance or compassion?

Your love was deep and melting

And mine warm and ferocious

Gliding through even the darkest

and lightest delicacies of the divine

altruistic flesh of ours hidden

within the ribs

And for now...

When I'm losing myself to be yours

My heart has frozen

For your cold.

Moments of joy could have happened

If my rage and your patience were equals

I owe this tiny tint of red thing

To my beloved queen

The owner of this core

To keep this in hers

Forever and ever and ever

Melting in your heart

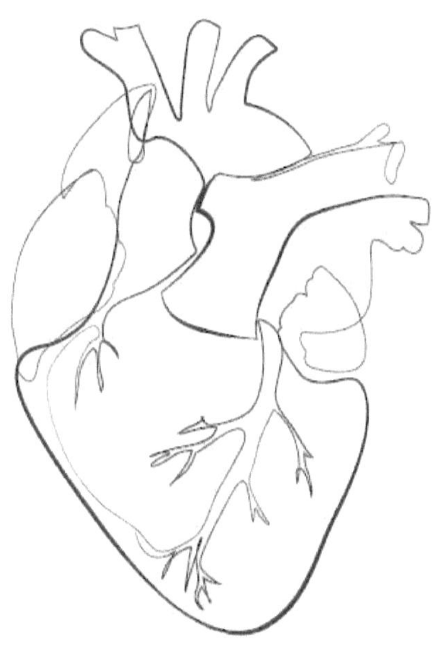

To be eternally yours"

People walking past her

Still, witness the perpetual miracle of

Love and passion

Where a tiny tint of red thing

Is safely kept

Enclosed in a large continental glacier

Where the ice and fire live

And where eternal love abide

That even the god of death

Would dare to touch.

20. What if they had a love story…

"May these warm rays of mine

Hug those green fields of yours

Giving hope to even the tiny droplets found"

Says the sun

"My days are shining

Cause of you

But the sparkle in my eyes

Are meant for the moon" Says

the earth.

All the images used within are not created by the writer

21. Oubaitori

The tides are above the sea

They are flying in the sky

And I'm still in the oceans

picking up the stones

Looking far away at them

Hoping my stones would shine one day

When they all will come in search of it

And I would fly above them all

With merry in my heart

Humbled and joyed

May that day be not far

away

And I know that I have my

own page and pace

That tells a different story

To many different audiences

22. Cynosure

I treasure myself

To the most

Without a pinch of mistrust

Even in the slightest.

You acquainted me with that

Cause there were none

To feed me love

When you were gone.

I devote myself

Without a fight

Thrashing on my insecurities

Welcoming it with more passion

Than I give it to my fellow little wings.

We fought all the way

To get lost

And to live a full life of myself

Which I was afraid to live on

As I always hid myself

All the images used within are not created by the writer

behind my timidities.

You taught me how

The loss of a man

Would take you to a brighter era of life

You taught me how

To sail upon the salty ocean of your eyes

Vibing to the triumph of yourself

To sing the song of loving

YOURSELLFFFF! ......

23. Shinki-itten

Nix is mint

All exist the same

Nonetheless, everything feels fresh

Numbness of infants

Cuddling up the tides of inner peace

Tryna reach the blue temples above

Peeking through the vintage windows

I see a lot, a lot and more

Mumbling on the bubbles of

your present of presence

Waving peek-a-boo on me

Iced Droplets of salty almond water

Looking upon me with Kalon

Withered flower plants probing for their

forgotten time tales

A lot I see, a lot I see

Change is not what I see

Yet it is all that I see

Always the same though distinct

Same tides, same wind
Same land, same me

And all and all

Is undoubtedly different

24. Loss

Your loss was my victory

Victory of winning myself

Beginning of a new era

Of moulding myself

Loving myself unconditionally

Without the help of an external force

Resolving my mental phase

To the pace of ease

Triumph over the

Ocean of scars laid by you

Loss that turned the way

Away from darkness

25. Verdict of troth

Every verdict

Is a troth

That I owe you

My core and soul

That I'll abide by your shores

Wandering through the silent breeze

This melody of us

Will be sung forever and ever

26. Melody of Diamonds

Versatile in the moonlight,

Diving through the ocean of dreams,

Speaking a hundred words,

I would like to open up to you.

The white rays of shine,

Asking to play with them,

And I wish to look at the innocence

sparkling in your eyes,

Pearls of love being chanted on me.

The voice of butterflies that I hear,

Saying to feel the moment.

Would you kill me with that stare of fresh

love living in those di almonds,

Or am I dying by myself

Being a melting melody inside them?

27. Valentine

Pretty morning

Pretty sunshine

And I remember of you making my days
shine

Sweet memory

That I will hold up to my heart

Like a valentine

But still with grief

Something that was real

Yet something that was fake

Was seen in you...

28. To the shore

If I could hold this breath a bit longer

To see your smile for the last time.

My soul would be a dreamer

That wanders in your dreams

Taking all your melancholies

To the shore of mine

Turning it to songs of joy

That will never down your smile.

If I could hold this breath a little longer

That I could make my last wish

When all I wish for

Is your gentle heart smile

That never failed to hug my heart

With pure emotions of love.

If this was a dream

And I could walk all the roads toward our
life

Hand in hand

Eyes and eyes

Heart to heart

With every wish I have

29. Little things

What else can I hold

In my heart

Than your face and memories

Blurred and burnt

By the beans of bees

That took us apart

Candles from the moon

Pearls from the ocean

Roses from the heaven

You ain't brought me all...

Yet you brought me all

All and all and all

Purest form of love

Divine feel of fulfilment of oneself

Silent rains of commitment.

You brought me flowers

With my name written on every petal

That you plucked from the deepest land of
your heart

Which no one could ever see.

And I saw a land where only I lived

Which predicted me with promises of fences
for no intruders

More Books from the Author

Poetry

Short Story Collection

Some books are worth reading for. And would you recommend this book to someone you love or someone who loves reading?

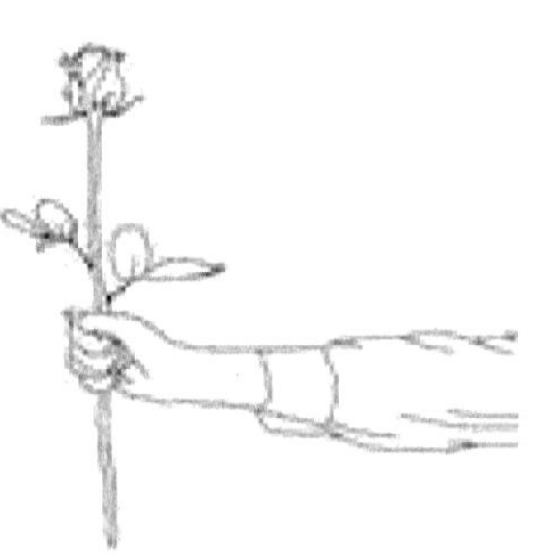

9 798889 961158 2